DREAM SCHEMES

The Spirit of the West

N214AU

404

DREAM SCHEMES

Exotic Airliner Art

Stuart Spicer

Motorbooks International
Publishers & Wholesalers

ACKNOWLEDGEMENTS

This book would not have been possible without the assistance and contributions of many people. In particular my grateful thanks are extended to the following: Andrew Abshier, Steve Anisman, Mike Axe, Will Blunt, Martyn Cartledge, Tony Cross (Braathens SAFE), Daryl Chapman, Peter Cooper, Mark Daniels, George Ditchfield, Michael Gallagher (Cathay Pacific), Clive Grant, Ryan Hales, Derek Hellman, Bob Holder, Peter May, Geoff McLaughlin (Air Nuigini), Yvonne Napper (ANA), Akinobu Okuda, Dominique Pernot (AOM), Olav Rheusius, Bob Schulman (Frontier), Robbie Shaw, Alistair Simpson, Tom Singfield, Phil Spicer, Jerry Stanick, Eric Trum, Richard Vandervord, Gabby Wilson, David Woodhead, Susan Yancey (Southwest) and Jan Young.

Unless credited otherwise all photographs are by the author.

This edition first published in 1997 by Motorbooks International, Publishers & Wholesalers, 792 Prospect Avenue, PO Box 1, Osceola, W154020, USA

Previously published in the UK in 1997 by Airlife Publishing Ltd

Library of Congress Cataloging-in-Publication Data Available

ISBN 0-7603-0442-4

Printed in Hong Kong

Aeroflot

In 1980 the Soviet Union were hosts to the Olympic Games and as a result Aeroflot became the Official Carrier; the 'Official' title was hardly surprising when you consider that Aeroflot were the only airline in that vast country covering eight and a half million square miles. A majority of their fleet, consisting entirely of Soviet-build types, carried the 'Official Olympic Carrier' titles throughout that year. When the Soviet Union fragmented into fifteen separate countries in 1991, breaking the state-owned aerial monopoly, Aeroflot became a much more streamlined operation. Within four years over five hundred airlines had been created. Today Aeroflot is no longer entirely dependent on Soviet types, and an Airbus A310, a Boeing 767 and a DC-10 can be seen flying in Aeroflot colours. The Tu-154 first entered service with Aeroflot in November 1971 and over six hundred are believed to have been delivered to Aeroflot; today fewer than thirty remain in service with the airline. Illustrated is Tupolev Tu-154B-2, CCCP-85375, which was seen at Prague, Czechoslovakia in May 1980.

Aero Union

Although not an airline, Aero Union, a fire-bombing operator based at Chico, California, painted one of their DC-4s into a bicentennial scheme to coincide with the celebrations in America in 1976. Accepted on charge by the USAAF as a C54D-1-DC, serial 42-72442, on 31 January 1945, the aircraft went to the RAF as KL997, where it was known as a Skymaster I. In July 1946 it was returned to the USA where the USN flew the aircraft as an R5D-3 Bu.No. 91994. In July 1970 the aircraft was retired to Davis-Monthan storage yard where it sat until Aero Union acquired the aircraft in December 1974 and converted it to an air-tanker. On 13 December 1976 it was registered N76AU from N62296 and painted in a patriotic scheme which was worn for several years. During 1990 Aero Union wound down their DC-4 operations as they converted to P2 Neptune and P3 Orion users. N76AU was transformed into its original C-54 guise as 272442, named *Santa Monica Maid*, and sold to join the American warbird circuit. It was seen in the hot sunny southern California sunshine during October 1978 awaiting its next fire-fighting call.

Air Atlantique

Air Atlantique commenced operations as an air taxi operator in 1969 under the name General Aviation, changing their name to Air Atlantique in 1975. In 1985 the DC-3 celebrated its fiftieth anniversary and the airline commemorated the milestone with some appropriate artwork on one of their own DC-3s, G-AMSV. This aircraft started life in 1944 as 44-76488, a C-47B Skytrain with the USAAF, before being diverted to the RAF where it became KN397. By 1952 it had passed into civilian hands as G-AMSV and earned its keep with various owners before Air Atlantique acquired the aircraft in March 1982. It is still in use today as part of a fleet of eleven Dakotas on passenger and cargo charters, as required. It is seen here while attending an airshow at Münster, Germany in May 1985. The legend '50th Anniversary 1935–1985' was added to the tail markings shortly afterwards.

Air Canada – Hong Kong

Air Canada was originally incorporated as Trans-Canada Airlines, a wholly-owned subsidiary of the Canadian National Railways, who were themselves wholly-owned by the Canadian government. In 1977 it became wholly-owned by the government and has been privatised since July 1989. Its current network, with the help of its own subsidiary airlines, offers flights to one hundred and twenty destinations including eight in Europe and eleven in the Caribbean and Asia. One of the latest additions to the network is Hong Kong, which started in mid-1995, and to promote this the airline added titles to one of its three Boeing 747-400 Combis, C-GAGL. The titles on the starboard nose read 'Yves and I are going to Hong Kong', while the port side was translated into French, reading 'Yves et moi partons pour Hong Kong'. The aircraft was seen at Heathrow in October 1995.

(SPA Photography).

Air Canada – Children's Miracle Network

In late 1995 Air Canada rolled out two of their A320 aircraft in special schemes. The first to appear, on 25 November, was A320-211 C-FDRP, which was graced with a row of smiling children's faces above the windows along the length of the fuselage in honour of Air Canada's sponsorship of the Children's Miracle Network of Canada, an organisation supporting hospitals for children.
(Mark Daniels)

Air France

Even the Hot-Rod, Concorde, has got in on the special scheme act in what must surely be the ultimate flying billboard. On 2 April 1996 Pepsi launched 'Project Blue', a £330 million promotion of a new blue can for its cola drinks; £125,000 of the budget went towards the painting of an Air France Concorde, F-BTSD, in an all-over blue scheme with the Pepsi name on the nose and wings. Departing from London–Gatwick after an £8 million press conference the aircraft undertook a brief tour of Europe and the Middle East visiting Dublin, Stockholm, Paris–Charles de Gaulle, Beirut, Dubai, Jeddah, Cairo, Milan and Madrid before returning to Paris–Orly on 9 April where a similar bill would see the aircraft returned to its standard Air France colours. To prevent the paint from peeling in the high temperatures encountered at high speeds the aircraft was restricted to just three Mach 1 supersonic flights of no more than fifteen minutes each in length. The aircraft was seen shortly before its departure from Gatwick. *(M.J. Axe)*

Air New Zealand

Air New Zealand began operations in 1940
as Tasman Empire Airways (TEAL), with
flying boat services to Australia. The
domestic carrier, New Zealand National
Airways Corporation, was formed in 1947.
In 1978 New Zealand's then government-
owned international and domestic airlines
were merged under the name Air New
Zealand. The inaugural flight of the airline's
service from Auckland to London took place
on 26 August 1982, and for a year Boeing
747-219B, ZK-NZV, one of a five-strong
fleet, wore 'London – All The Way With The
Pacific's Number One' titles, together with a
London horseguard, on the nose of the
aircraft. *(Clive Grant)*

Air Niugini

Air Niugini are a government-owned airline formed on 1 November 1973, with initial help from Ansett, TAA and Qantas, as the national airline of Papua New Guinea. Their original fleet of twenty aircraft comprised twelve DC-3s and eight Fokker Friendship F27s. Boeing 707 and 727s arrived soon after and international routes were added to the domestic roster. On 27 November 1984 Air Niugini leased from Trans Australia Airlines an A300B4-203 P2-ANG and C/N134, which had previously flown with Condor as D-AITA, pending the delivery of their own A300. This aircraft, known as 'Big Bird', appeared in the Raggiana Bird of Paradise scheme, the national symbol of Papua New Guinea, until it was returned to TAA where it became VH-TAA. Today the slightly smaller fleet of twelve aircraft fly routes around the Pacific with destinations including Australia, Hong Kong and Indonesia. 'Big Bird' was seen at a murky Kingsford-Smith Airport, Sydney in October 1988.

Alaska Airlines

During 1995 Alaska Airlines added comic-book-style speech bubbles to some of their MD-82 and MD-83s with the comments 'Swell' and 'Good Choice' extending from the passenger windows while the Eskimo on the tail could be seen saying 'Thanks'. The comments were part of a promotional campaign. One of these talking planes, MD-83 N933AS, was seen at Phoenix in March 1996. These were not the first special markings applied to Alaska's aircraft however: during the early seventies the airline's fleet wore four different tail schemes representing Russian Alaska (featuring Russian Church 'onion domes'), Gold Rush Alaska (1890s prospector), Native Alaska (bird totem) and Eskimo Alaska (Eskimo). In 1976 the airline standardised its colours retaining the Eskimo face but changing the sullen expression to the smiling face that is worn on the tails today.

All Nippon Airways

All Nippon Airways started life in February 1954 when the Japan Helicopter and Aeroplane Transport Company, the forerunner of ANA, flew a De Havilland Dove from Tokyo–Osaka. In under forty years the airline flew its 500 millionth passenger, and to celebrate the passing of the milestone on 12 August 1992 ANA placed adverts in several Japanese newspapers for a design competition to paint a special scheme for a Boeing 747. The winning entry, from over twenty thousand submitted, was based on a whale and was designed by twelve-year-old Yukie Ogaki. Boeing painted the whale design, which used twelve colours and four hundred gallons of paint, and the aircraft was christened *Marine Jumbo*. The aircraft, a 569-seat Boeing 747-481D (D for Domestic and without winglets), JA8963, arrived at Tokyo–Haneda Airport from Seattle on 2 September 1993. Such was the popularity of the aircraft, with passengers and at airports, that it was decided to paint a Boeing 767-381, JA8579, to serve domestic airports that were unable to accept a 747. Again delivered from Seattle to Haneda, *Marine Jumbo Junior* arrived on 4 December 1993. Both aircraft had a dedicated maintenance team to keep the aircraft fully serviceable and the paintwork tidy. Although they were originally intended to return to normal ANA colours after one year, their popularity and the Kobe earthquake in January 1995 brought a reprieve for both aircraft. Between them 1,700,000 passengers were flown by the time *Marine Jumbo Junior* stepped down on 22 May 1995, and *Marine Jumbo* completed its duties on 31 May 1995. *(Akinobu Okuda) (ANA)*

America West – Teamwork

Emerging from three years under Chapter 11 bankruptcy protection on 25 August 1994, America West held an in-house competition for employees' children to design a scheme for an aircraft to convey 'teamwork'. The winner from the four hundred entries was eleven-year-old Ann Rogan, daughter of 737 captain John Rogan. Nicknamed 'Romper Room' the winning design was rolled out on Boeing 737-2S7, N902AW, at Phoenix on 29 August 1994. The aircraft was snapped as it departed Phoenix on 27 March 1996.

The close-up shows some of the characters representing all levels of the employee structure.

America West – Phoenix Suns

America West take a keen interest in Arizona-based sports teams and are the Official Airline of the Arizona Diamondbacks baseball team and the Phoenix Suns basketball team. The airline have painted one aircraft, Boeing 757-225 N907AW, in a Phoenix Suns scheme which was rolled out at Phoenix on 16 May 1994. The aircraft is different inside as well as outside: with so many tall guys in the basket ball team America West have fitted the aircraft with just eighty-six seats to give them the much-needed extra legroom. The aircraft was seen at Phoenix in March 1996.
(Author (Phoenix Suns))

America West – Nevada, Arizona and Ohio Flags

Patriotic liveries seem to be popular with America West as they have three Boeing 757s painted in state flag colours. The first to appear was 757-2G7, N915AW, which was rolled out on 14 December 1994 wearing a livery based on the Nevada state flag. The scheme prominently features the state motto 'Battle Born'. This was followed by 757-23A, N916AW, which features the airline's home state flag of Arizona. The aircraft is named *City of Tucson* on the starboard side and *City of Phoenix* on the port side. Joining these two on 1 October 1995 was 757-2S7, N905SW, which wears the colours of the Ohio state flag. The aircraft is named *City of Columbus*. All three aircraft were photographed at America West's home base of Phoenix, Arizona. *Arizona (Author), Nevada (Robbie Shaw), Ohio (Ryan Hales), overleaf Ohio (Author), Arizona (Ryan Hales)*

American Trans Air

American Trans Air were formed in August 1973 to manage the Ambassador Travel Club. In the years since their formation they have steadily grown and today operate a fleet of Boeing 727, Boeing 737 and Lockheed TriStars on scheduled and charter passenger and cargo services. In early 1994 two of the thirteen TriStars with the airline, N190AT and N191AT, had 'Pleasant Hawaiian Holidays' titles applied along the fuselage in place of the airline's name, and they are dedicated to the Hawaiian routes. On 15 November 1995 the airline introduced a new tropical scheme which is gradually being applied to its aircraft. N191AT (right) was photographed in March 1996 wearing the Hawaiian titling.
(Derek Hellman)

N191AT (below) was photographed in March 1996 wearing the Hawaiian titling.
(Mark Daniels)

Ansett
Established in 1935 by R.M. Ansett as Ansett Airways, they were renamed Ansett Transport Industries in 1946 and taken over by News Corporation and TNT Limited in 1979. In 1987 Eastwest Airlines and Kendell Airlines were acquired and during 1994 its subsidiary airlines Ansett WA, Ansett Express and Eastwest were fully absorbed into the Ansett infrastructure. In early 1995 a Boeing 737-376, VH-CZA, was painted in a special livery to commemorate the 100th anniversary of Banjo Patterson's 'Waltzing Matilda' folk song, Australia's unofficial national anthem. The artwork was painted by an artist who painted nose-art during World War II *(Author's Collection)*

AOM French Airlines

AOM French Airlines were formed in 1991 following a merger between Minerva and Air Outre Mer, to become one of Europe's largest private airlines. Flying from Paris–Orly Airport they utilise a fleet of eight MD-83 and thirteen DC-10 aircraft flying domestic routes as well as long-haul to the French West Indies, Australia, South and North America. In early 1995 it was decided that an aircraft would be painted to add some colour to the fleet. A competition was run, in conjuction with a Marseille newspaper, with six thousand entry forms sent to children with the brief 'Draw Me An Aeroplane'. Four thousand entries were returned and the eventual winner was ten-year-old Alizée Jacotey. Her design was then applied to MD-83, F-GGMB, and the aircraft was named *Alizée* in her honour. Unveiled in June 1995, the aircraft has been so popular that it has been decided to paint a DC-10 in the same scheme. *(SPA Photography)*

Asiana

Unlike Korean Air, whose ancestry can be traced back to the start of South Korea's existence in 1948, Asiana's history is somewhat shorter by some fifty years. Formed in 1988 as Seoul Air International, their creation came about as a result of the Korean government's decision to create a second flag carrier in the country. Serving eleven South Korean cities the airline also flies to eighteen cities in Japan, China, south-east Asia and the USA. During 1994 their fleet, of about forty aircraft, flew with 'Visit Korea Year 1994' underneath the Asiana titles. Boeing 747-48E, HL7415, (above) was captured on 17 April 1994 while on approach to Tokyo's Narita Airport. *(Akinobu Okuda)*

During 1995 the Asiana fleet began promoting Korea's bid to host the World Cup football competition in the year 2002. Boeing 747-48E, HL7416, was seen wearing the relevant titles at Narita Airport, Tokyo in May 1995. *(Akinobo Okuda)*

Braniff

The Braniff name has led a checkered history since it was formed back in 1927 by two brothers, Paul and Tom Braniff. Based in Dallas the airline survived until 13 May 1982 when it went bankrupt, owing $733 million, following the deregulation of the US airline system. Its seventy-one aircraft made an impressive, but sad, sight as they all sat stored at Dallas–Fort Worth Airport. Rising from the ashes the airline re-formed in March 1984 and lasted until November 1989 after filing for bankruptcy two months earlier. A further resurrection a year later saw operations commence once again, but it was not to prove third time lucky and the airline went bankrupt again in July 1992. On 1 November 1965 the airline introduced their 'Flying Colours' image when a BAC 1-11 and a Boeing 727 were rolled out in orange and lavender schemes respectively. These were the first of seven different colours that the aircraft were to appear in. The illustrations show a few of the variations in the colours and schemes adopted during the airline's second and third periods. *N8856E Blue (Martyn Cartledge), N531PA Purple and N458BN Burgundy (Author's Collection)*

Braathens SAFE – Sommerflyet 1993

For several years, the Norwegian airline Braathens SAFE have applied a 'Sommerflyet' (Summerflight) scheme to one of their aircraft. The 1993 scheme, carried on Boeing 737-500 LN-BRX, featured around twenty drawings by schoolchildren following a competition on the theme 'planes'. The names and ages of each child were also added to each drawing. The aircraft is seen here during a visit to Gatwick in April 1993. *(Robbie Shaw)*

Braathens SAFE – Sommerflyet 1994
Braathens' annual 'Sommerflyet' schemes are intended to highlight seasonal fares on the airline's domestic routes. For 1994 the airline called upon the services of their own marketing department to design a summer scheme. The design, which featured coloured stripes and balloons, was then given to the airline's technical division at Stavanger who transferred the design on to eighty square metres of adhesive material. The aircraft, Boeing 737-500 LN-BRJ, is one of twenty 500 series aircraft in the fleet and was captured on film during a visit to Gatwick in July of that year. *(Robbie Shaw)*

Braathens – Olympiaflyet 1994
For a brief period at the end of 1994 Braathens painted this Boeing 737-500, LN-BRJ, in an 'Olympiaflyet' scheme. The markings were first unveiled on 12 November 1994 and the aircraft made its last appearance on 3 January 1995. LN-BRJ would seem to be the airline's dedicated special scheme aircraft as it was also the 1994 and 1995 'Sommerflyet' plane.
(Robbie Shaw)

Braathens – 1995 Sommerflyet
The 1995 'Sommerflyet' scheme was designed by schoolchildren and represents images of its route network in Norway. The aircraft selected was once again Boeing 737-500 LN-BRJ one of twenty-nine Boeing 737s, in their all-737 fleet. Like the 1993 'Sommerflyet' scheme the authors' names and ages appear alongside their artwork.
(Robbie Shaw)

Braathens SAFE – 50th Anniversary

Based in Oslo, Braathens SAFE was formed in 1946 by the Braathens Shipping Company to operate long-haul charters to South America and the Far East (hence SAFE) using Douglas DC-4 aircraft. Today the airline operates scheduled services in Europe, which accounts for about seventy per cent of their annual turnover, and charters to destinations all over Europe and the Canary Islands. The fleet consists of about thirty Boeing 737 aircraft with a mix of 200, 300 and 500 models. In 1996 the airline celebrated its fiftieth anniversary and applied an appropriate logo to its aircraft in recognition of the occasion. Boeing 737-400, LN-BRB, was photographed in April 1996 shortly after the markings first appeared.
(SPA Photography)

British Airways – The World's Biggest Offer

Following the Gulf War in 1990 British Airways ran a promotion to encourage people to fly again. Under the banner 'The World's Biggest Offer' 50,000 free tickets were offered on their aircraft for flights to be taken on 23 April 1991. People pre-booked on that day were given a voucher for a free flight at another time. One or more of several types of the fleet were treated to the banner and included the Boeing 737, 747, 757, 767, DC-10 and BAE ATP. Boeing 737-236, G-BGDS, *River Severn* was seen preparing for departure from Heathrow on 26 April 1991.

British Airways – Fly New Club Europe

Airlines are constantly striving to improve the level of service they can offer their customers as the battle between airlines for passengers seems to get ever more competitive and cut-throat. In 1994 British Airways began upgrading their Club Class service in Europe by fitting wider business-class seats. Ten aircraft were selected to carry the message around the airline's European network with five Boeing 757 and five 767 aircraft displaying 'Fly New Club Europe' along the fuselage. Seen (below) on final approach to Heathrow on 5 May 1995 was Boeing 757-236, G-BIKV *Raglan Castle*. The markings were worn for about one year.

This close-up (left) on a Boeing 757 clearly shows off the 'Fly New Club Europe' logo worn on ten British Airways aircraft in late 1994 and throughout 1995.
(SPA Photography)

British Airways – Paint-a-Plane

In the months leading up to Christmas 1994, British Airways ran a nationwide competition for children up to the age of eleven and from eleven to fourteen to 'Paint-A-Plane' depicting Christmas using a maximum of five colours. The competition was won by ten-year-old Rebecca Rees from Swansea whose design was worn on the starboard side, and Lisa Falconer, aged fourteen from Aberdeen, whose night-time drawing was featured on the port side. The chosen aircraft, Boeing 737-236, G-BKYK, was unveiled on 18 December 1994 and departed Heathrow carrying gifts to Romania. The aircraft wore the two prize-winning schemes through the twelve days of Christmas before returning to the paintshop on 6 January 1995 to revert to its normal British Airways colours. Ten-year-old Rebecca Rees's painting was one of two winners of the British Airways 'Paint-A-Plane' competition and was seen on the gate at Manchester Airport in early January 1995. *(Peter May)*

The port side of the 'Paint-a-Plane' Boeing 737-236, G-BKYK, (right) saw the artwork of fourteen-year-old Lisa Falconer applied. The scheme was worn for fewer than three weeks. *(SPA Photography)*

British Airways – Dream Flight

In October 1992 British Airways applied additional markings to their Boeing 747-136, G-AWNE *Derwent Water*, as part of a special flight which took disabled children on a trip to Orlando. Named 'Dreamflight' the exercise was repeated again in 1995 when Boeing 747-136, G-BDPV *Blea Water*, was the chosen recipient of the titles.

The aircraft is seen departing London–Heathrow in October 1995. British Airways currently operate about sixty Boeing 747 aircraft in a fleet of some two hundred aircraft. *(SPA Photography)*

British Airways – International Children's Conference

In recent years British Airways have applied special markings to various aircraft to promote their involvement in a variety of projects. On 14 September 1995 Boeing 747-436, G-CIVB, was rolled out wearing 'International Children's Conference' titles along its fuselage with a suitably painted tail. The conference was held in Eastbourne between 25 and 28 October 1995 and British Airways carried the delegates free of charge. The markings were worn for about two months. The illustration shows a close-up of the tail as the aircraft was caught lining up for departure from Heathrow on 2 October 1995.

British Air Ferries and Dan Air

Political parties have often been known to charter an aircraft to maximise their time on the campaign trail during election periods; 1992 was no exception when two of the British parties chartered an aircraft each to ferry their aides and assembled press corps to strategic, or marginal, constituencies around the country. The Labour party leader Neil Kinnock used the services of British Air Ferries BAe 146-200, G-BTIA, while the Liberal Democratic party leader, Paddy Ashdown, employed a HS748-2A, G-BIUV of Dan Air. Neither airline now exists as British Air Ferries changed their name to British World Airlines in 1993 and the ailing Dan Air was acquired by British Airways in October 1992 for one pound and a net £35 million to clear its creditors and obtain its assets, which included thirty-eight aircraft. Both aircraft were photographed at Manchester during April 1992. *(George Ditchfield)*

British Midland

British Midland can trace their ancestry back to 1938 when it was established as Air Schools. Further name changes followed in 1948 (Derby Aviation), 1959 (Derby Airways), and finally in 1964 the British Midland name was adopted. Today the airline has grown to become the UK's second largest airline flying an extensive European network. Two more cities were added on 29 October 1995 when services commenced to Zürich, with four daily flights, and Prague, with one daily flight. Promoting these new destinations the airline applied a different message on each side of the aircraft with one side stating 'Heathrow–Zürich Four Times Daily' while the other read 'Heathrow–Zürich–Prague from October 29th'. Illustrated are a Fokker 100 and Boeing 737-500 showing the 'Heathrow-Zürich Four Times Daily' message. *(SPA Photography) (Martyn Cartledge)*

Canadian

A totally different special scheme appeared in July 1993 when Canadian applied enlarged employee signatures all over DC-10-30 N6150Z for a television commercial. The aircraft was one of two leased from Potomac on a power-by-the-hour basis and did not fly in this guise. In 1995 the process was repeated again when the airline ran a 'Name the Aircraft' contest which resulted in DC-10-30, C-FRCE, being named *Spirit of Canadian/L'Esprit de Canadien*. The signatures of all of the employees who entered were then transferred into decal form and a Canadian DC-10 was once again transformed into a signature billboard. On this occasion the aircraft entered service and has been seen all over the Canadian network. It was photographed in March 1996 while operating into London–Heathrow. *(SPA Photography)*

Casino Express

Casino Express are a charter operator founded in 1988 and based in Elko, Nevada. Their charters mainly take gamblers to cities like Las Vegas and Reno. Three aircraft, Boeing 737-200s, have flown with the company: N456TM *King of Diamonds,* N457TM *Queen of Hearts* and EI-CJW *Ace of Clubs,* though this aircraft has now returned to the lessor. There have been several variations of the colours worn. Originally the heads had two eyes but this was deemed to look odd and the heads were revised to show just one. Later the scheme was revised again to move the colours from the top of the fuselage to the bottom. The illustrations show the first Queen scheme, seen in February 1993 and worn until the revised scheme was applied, and the new scheme as seen in December 1994. The King, seen in July 1994, also shows the current 'white top' scheme.

(Andrew Abshier)

Cathay Pacific

With world peace restored at the end of World War II in 1945 people were once again free to travel the world in safety and many new airlines were formed, often using surplus military aircraft. Hong Kong's Cathay Pacific was one such airline, formed on 24 September 1946 and starting life with a war surplus DC-3 costing $30,000, which became VR-HDB and was named *Betsy*. The first commercial flight was to Sydney, returning to Shanghai with a cargo of woollen goods. As the route network grew so did the fleet and Catalinas, DC-4s, DC-6s and Electras saw them through to the jet age

when, in 1962, the airline purchased a Convair 880. By 1967 the fleet was all jet and in the last thirty years the Boeing 707, TriStar and Boeing 747 have carried the Cathay name worldwide. During 1996 the airline celebrated its fiftieth birthday and a fiftieth anniversary logo was applied to the nose of all the aircraft. At the same time the airline is expanding with new aircraft joining the fleet in the form of the Airbus A330 and A340 and the Boeing 777. Boeing 747-476F, VR-HUK, one of the newer members of the fleet, was seen visiting Los Angeles in March 1996. *(Mark Daniels)*

Classic Air

DC-3 operator Classic Air are a Swiss-based charter and pleasure flight airline formed on 17 December 1985, coincidentally the fiftieth anniversary of the first flight of the prototype DC-3. Initially starting with one DC-3, HB-ISB, they soon added another when HB-ISC, previously N88YA, joined its partner in Switzerland in November 1986. Celebrating their tenth anniversary in 1995 the airline applied '10 Jahre' markings on its aircraft. HB-ISC, C/N 9995, is seen at Zürich in March 1995 wearing the birthday scheme.

Built in 1943 as a C-47A this particular aircraft served within the USA during World War II befre being released into the civilian market in August 1948 where it passed through the hands of several operators before being purchased by Classic Air. Note that this aircraft has panoramic windows. *(Olav Rheusius)*

Crossair – 700th Anniversary Swiss Federation

Crossair, a Swiss regional and domestic airline, was established in 1975 as a pilot training and air taxi company flying a range of aircraft that included a Cessna Citation and two Piper Cubs. In 1978 the company changed their name from Business Flyers Basel AG to Crossair and concentrated their services on businessmen. Crossair slowly developed and in 1984 became the launch customer of the Saab SF-430A. In 1991 the Swiss Federation celebrated its 700th anniversary and Crossair joined in the celebrations by running a painting competition for children. The winner was ten-year-old Giacomo Fiscalini from Brissago and his winning design was applied to one of their Saab 340As, HB-AHD. Although it was only meant to retain the scheme for one year it continues to fly in these markings. To celebrate the 700th anniversary of the Swiss Federation in 1991, Crossair painted one of their thirty-four Saab 340s in this special scheme following a competition for school-children.

It was photographed basking in the sun (below) in August 1992 and seen at a later date on a visit to Manchester (right) while on lease to the Scottish airline, Business Air. *(via M.J. Cartledge/George Ditchfield)*

Crossair – Phantom of the Opera

On 2 July 1995 Crossair unveiled its latest Saab 2000 when the aircraft, painted in the colours of *The Phantom of the Opera,* went into service by flying from Basle to Heathrow. The aircraft was then used on the carrier's European network to promote the show. The scheme reflected Crossair's involvement as a major sponsor of the Andrew Lloyd-Webber musical which opened in Basle, the company's head-quarters, on 2 October 1995. The aircraft involved, HB-IZK, wore a different scheme on both sides and was the tenth to be delivered to Crossair who now have a fleet of fifteen Saab 2000s. In late 1995 it was announced that the airline were installing shoulder height (when sitting) windows in the toilets of these aircraft, presumably so that if nature called the views of the Alps could still be enjoyed! The starboard side was seen in March 1996 while visiting Zürich while the port side and head-on shots were seen at London–Heathrow the following month. *(Olav Rheusius(Starboard Side))(SPA Photography (Port & Head-on,))*

46

Crossair – McDonalds

Crossair's latest scheme involves a collaboration between Hotelplan, a Swiss tour operator, and McDonald's fast food chain. Making its first appearance on 29 March 1996 the 161-seat MD-83, HB-IUH, has been dubbed 'The Ketchup Flight' and 'McPlane.' The aircraft will be used to promote family travel and was seen at Zürich shortly after entering service in its new scheme. *(Olav Rheusius)*

Delta Air Lines

Based in Atlanta, Georgia, venue for the 1996 Olympic Games, Delta Air Lines secured the franchise to be the Official Olympic Airline for the games. On 27 July 1995 the airline rolled out Boeing 767-232, N102DA, (below) in a special scheme to mark their Official Airline status. The basic scheme will become the airline's new scheme. Named *Spirit of Delta,* the aircraft was originally presented to the airline by their employees on 15 December 1982 and was the airline's first 767. An MD-11 was also painted into the colours. The first application of the Olympic logo appeared on the engines of Delta's new MD-90s, as seen on the first aircraft to wear the Olympic sticker, N902DA, (centre) in November 1994. However, this was short-lived and the MD-90s, along with the rest of Delta's 480-strong fleet, have a simplified sticker placed on the forward fuselage of each aircraft. The special scheme was seen at its home base in August 1995 while the Official Carrier nose logo was seen on Boeing 767, N644DN, (top right) at Phoenix in March 1996. *(Jerry Stanick (MD-90 engine)) (Jerry Stanick (Special Scheme)) (Author (Nose logo))*

Eastwest
New South Wales-based Eastwest Airlines began operations in June 1947 with a seven-passenger Avro Anson flying from Tamworth to Sydney. Other early duties included freight, air ambulance and crop-dusting. Lockheed Hudsons, Dakotas and Fokker F27s saw the airline through to 1990 when two BAe 146-300s flew from Hatfield to Australia to join the airline. During the eighties and into the nineties Eastwest added additional markings to a selection of aircraft to promote its flights to various holiday destinations. The second of Eastwest's eight BAe 146s, VH-EWJ, was seen at Sydney in February 1993 wearing 'Hamilton Islands Reef Adventure' titles. A subsidiary of Ansett Australia since 1987, Eastwest were fully absorbed into Ansett during 1994. *(Robbie Shaw)*

El Al Israel Airlines

El Al Israel Airlines is as old as the country itself, having been formed in 1948 when Israel became an independent state from Palestine. Throughout the 1990s the airline has flown an all-Boeing fleet comprising 737, 747, 757 and 767 models. During 1995 its aircraft appeared with 'Jerusalem 3000' logos, celebrating David making the city the capital of a united Jewish Kingdom in 1,000 BC, and promoting the 'Israel Tennis Center'. One of these aircraft was Boeing 747-458, 4X-EZA, and was caught wearing both stickers in October 1995. *(SPA Photography)*

Frontier Airlines

Frontier Airlines' start-up on 5 July 1994 took advantage of Continental's dramatic downsizing of their Denver operations from over one hundred and fifty daily flights to just thirteen and vacating fifty-one of its fifty-four destinations. Seeing the gap in the market Frontier were formed and selected twelve of the void sectors to create their service network. The original Frontier Airlines ceased operations in 1986 following their acquisition by People Express. Many of those original employees now work for the new Frontier. The airline's marketing theme, 'The Spirit of the West', is seen on the tails of their seven Boeing 737 aircraft in the form of twenty-one-foot-high decals of western wildlife. Each decal originates from a 35mm photo that has been computer-enlarged 'a zillion times'. From there the photo is divided into forty sections, each of which becomes a four-foot-by-three-foot 'tile' backed with high-tech adhesive. A different image is worn on both sides of the tail. Boeing 737-201, N205AU, was leased from USAir in September 1994 and features a wide-eyed racoon on the port tail and a red fox on the starboard side. It was the fourth aircraft to join the fleet.

N212US is another aircraft leased from USAir. A 201 model, it features a mountain ram on the port side and a grazing bison on the starboard side.

One of Frontier's first aircraft was Boeing 737-201, N214AU, which is another USAir example leased in July 1994. It carries a Bambi-like fawn and a mountain goat on its port and starboard sides respectively.

The airline has five 737-201s on lease from USAir including N217US which joined Frontier in October 1994 and shows a cougar with its cub and a bald eagle.

One of Frontier's start-up aircraft, and the second to join the fleet, was 737-201, N207AU, which displays a howling coyote on the port tail and a cuddly bear cub on the starboard side.

Frontier have two 737-300s on strength including EI-CHH, a 737-317 which features a mallard in flight on the port tail and a galloping stallion on the starboard side.

Leased in October 1995, Frontier's seventh aircraft is a 373-301, N578US, and shows a pair of polar bears, Klondike and Snow, which were born in Denver Zoo. The port side shows a pair of fox cubs.

A line-up of tails at Frontier's home base, Denver International Airport, shows a selection of the wildlife tails worn by the airline.

Garuda

Garuda Indonesia is one of the Orient's largest airlines, serving the archipelago of about 6,000 islands and 180 million people. The airline started in 1950 with a single DC-3 and was jointly formed by the government and KLM, and in 1954 the government exercised its right to buy the KLM share. Early types operated by the airline also include the Catalina, DH114 Heron and Lockheed Electra before the Convair CV990 joined the fleet in 1963 to make Garuda a jet operator. Today the airline operates to all corners of the world using an all-jet fleet. In 1990/91 its aircraft wore 'Visit Indonesia Year 1991' titles.

Boeing 747-2U3B was photographed in these markings in February 1990. *(Tom Singfield)*

Japan Airlines – Dream Express

In a second attempt to counter ANA's *Marine Jumbo* and *Marine Jumbo Junior*, which had been popular with children and achieved high load factors, JAL introduced the 'Dream Express' scheme to promote family discount fares, family-orientated tours and Disneyland–Tokyo. Unveiled on 1 August 1994, two Boeing 747-146B (SR)s, JA8142 and JA8170, and three Boeing 767-346s, JA8397, JA8398 and JA8399, were painted in the 'Disney on Tour' scheme for the year-long campaign. Cabin staff were decked out with Disney character aprons, though apparently the stewardesses mutinied when asked to wear Minnie Mouse ears. Both sides of the aircraft carried different designs. The main photo (below) shows the starboard side of Boeing 767-436, JA8399, and was photographed at Tokyo-Haneda on 24 February 1995. The aircraft was returend to the normal JAL scheme during November 1995. The tail photo (right) shows a closeup of the aircraft. It is shown here on Boeing 747-146B(SR/SUD), JA8170, at Tokyo-Haneda on 27 November 1994. *(Akinobu Okuda)*

Japan Airlines – Super Resort Express

After ANA unveiled their 'Marine Jumbo' design in September 1993, Japan Airlines' response was to launch the 'Super Resort Express' (SRE) scheme, which was intended to convey a tropical image, initially on their Honolulu route but later extended to their Asian and Pacific services. Meal services and uniforms extend the tropical theme. Two colour schemes, featuring hibiscus flowers and exotic birds, were applied to a total of eleven Boeing 747s and comprised a yellow/pink/red or a purple/red scheme. Two aircraft received an additional 'Okinawa', title to the SRE titles and fly a dedicated route between Tokyo and Okinawa. Japan Air Charter (JAZ), a subsidiary of JAL, also had two of its DC-10s similarly treated, flying from various airports in Japan to Honolulu.

The first service of the Super Resort Express was taken by Boeing 747, JA8111, on 4 June 1994 and flew from Tokyo–Narita to Honolulu. The aircraft was photographed shortly before the inaugural flight. *(Akinobu Okuda)*

Boeing 747-246B, JA8131, displays the
yellow Resort scheme and was seen on
approach to Hong Kong's Kai-Tak Airport.
(Daryl Chapman)

Boeing 747-246B, JA8111, has had an extra flower added behind the JAL titles since it first appeared in June 1994.
(Akinobu Okuda)

Two Super Resort Express Boeing 747's have 'Okinawa' added to their titles and fly a dedicated route between Tokyo and Okinawa.

Japan Airlines – J Birds

To give its MD-11s their own identity JAL have named each aircraft in the fleet after a bird and painted the bird on the fuselage and winglets of the aircraft. The aircraft are known as 'J Birds'. For the ornithologists they are named *Etopirica* (Tufted Puffin) JA8580, *Yairocho* (Fairy Pitta) '81, *Tancho* (Red Crowned Crane) '82, *Inuwashi* (Golden Eagle) '83, *Yanbarukuina* (Okinawa Rail) '84, *Yamataka* (Hodgson's Hawk Eagle) '85, *Kounotori* (White Stork) '86, *Noguchigera* (Pryer's Woodpecker) '87, *Ojirowashi* (White Tailed Eagle) '88, and *Raicho* (Rock Ptarmigan) '89. Illustrated is JA8586 *White Stork* which also wears the 'Unicef' and 'World City Expo' stickers. In a similar trait JAL are naming their Boeing 747-400s Flower Jets and 777s Star Jets after a constellation. *(Akinobu Okuda)*

Japan Airlines – Stickers

For over twenty-five years Japan Airlines have been the Official Airline or supporter of a number of causes and have displayed stickers to promote the fact. All of the fleet carry the 'We Support Unicef' sticker on the rear of both sides of the aircraft. The port side also wears 'Official Airline for Universiade '95 – Fukuoka', 'Official Airline for Nippon Love Goal–2002 World Cup Japan' or 'Official Airline for World City Expo Tokyo '96'. Shown are a couple of recent examples. *(SPA Photography)*

Korean Air

Like several other countries in the Asian sector, a year was selected as the year to visit that country; 1994 was the year that Korea wanted you to visit them and the aircraft of Korean Air let you know this when they carried the titles 'Visit Korea 94' on their aircraft. Korean Air was formed in 1962 as a successor to Korean National Airlines, which itself was formed in 1948 when South Korea declared itself an independent republic. Today the airline's fleet consists of numerous types and range from Piper PA-34 Senecas, which are used as trainers, to Airbus A300, Boeing 747 and McDonnell Douglas MD-11s.

Here, Korean Air's first MD-11, HL7371, one of five in the fleet (left), was seen taking a rest at Brisbane, Australia in December 1994 while Boeing 747-4B5(SCD), HL7482, is seen arriving at Frankfurt, Germany in June 1994.

(Author's collection/David Woodhead)

63

After the 1994 logo became obsolete it was replaced by another logo promoting Korea's dream of hosting the World Cup football competition in 2002, as seen on Airbus A300-622R, HL7288, (top) at Hong Kong in late 1995. *(Derek Hellman)*

For the 1988 Olympic Games, held in Seoul, Korean Air flew as the Official Airline of the games. Airbus A300F4-203 HL-7279, one of two cargo versions with the airline, was seen wearing the Olympic markings while visiting Tokyo's Narita Airport on 13 October 1988.

Kuwait Airways

Kuwait National Airways Corporation was formed in 1954 with three DC-3s flying routes around the Middle East. In 1963 Comet 4Cs joined the fleet and services were extended to London. Further jets were acquired in the form of the Hawker Siddeley Trident 1E and Boeing 707s. The Tridents were released in 1978 and two Boeing 747s were acquired which greatly increased the airline's range, and destinations as far away as Chicago and Manila were added. By mid-1990 twenty-three aircraft were flying to forty-two airports on four continents. That was until 2 August 1990 when Iraqi troops invaded Kuwait and the Gulf War started. During the conflict fifteen aircraft were stolen of which seven were destroyed. Allied forces rallied to the cause and Operation Desert Storm was fought to a victory, liberating Kuwait from Iraq on 26 February 1991. The war was not without its casualties: as well as the seven destroyed Kuwait aircraft, a KAF DC-9 and British Airways Boeing 747 were also lost and there were still 650 hostages being held captive or missing. So that these people are not forgotten, all Kuwait Airways aircraft wear a yellow ribbon and 'Do Not Forget Our POWs' on the fuselage. Boeing 747-269B, 9K-ADB, was out of the country when hostilities in Kuwait began. It wears the yellow ribbon and 'Do Not Forget Our POWs' reminder on the rear of the fuselage. *(SPA Photography)*

Photographed exactly one year after Kuwait's liberation Boeing 747-269B, 9K-ADB, wore the 'Do Not Forget Our POWs' behind the cockpit and was seen while visiting Manchester Airport. *(Peter May)*

Kuwait Airways fly one Boeing 727 in VIP configuration. This aircraft was captured during the Gulf War and spent a period of time in Oman before returning to Kuwait. It flies with its yellow sash displayed differently to the rest of the fleet and was seen at London–Heathrow in January 1996. *(SPA Photography)*

Lufthansa

The run-off for the prize of hosting the Olympic Games in the year 2000 was hotly contested with several countries battling it out. Lufthansa carried its country's message with 'Berlin 2000' stickers applied to most of its fleet. The sticker was barely noticeable on the larger aircraft but, as can be seen here on this Boeing 737-300, the motif is clearly visible. The aircraft, D-ABEE of Lufthansa Express, was seen on home soil at Düsseldorf in June 1993. The Lufthansa Express title was also adopted in 1993 to cover its European regional routes. Five years earlier Lufthansa aircraft wore markings denoting that they were the 'Official Carrier – UEFA 88 European Championships' as seen on Boeing 727-300 Advanced, D-ABKG. *(Author's Collection)*

Malaysia Airlines

Malaysia Airlines have undergone numerous name changes in their sixty years of existence. Established in 1937 operations did not commence until 1 May 1947. Formed as Malayan Airways by Straits Steamship, Ocean Steamship and Imperial Airways, they were renamed Malaysian airways in 1963 when Malaysia was formed. Further changes were Malaysia-Singapore Airlines in 1967, Malaysian Airlines Berhad in 1971 and Malaysian Airlines System in 1972. The final name change was in October 1987 when the present name, Malaysia Airlines, was adopted. Today the fleet consists of around one hundred aircraft and nine different types. In 1990 the aircraft wore 'Visit Malaysia Year 1990' to encourage tourism to the country. The exercise was repeated in 1994.

Boeing 737-2H6 Advanced was snapped at Singapore on 17 February 1990. *(Akinobu Okuda)*

DC-10-30 9M-MAT, one of ten with the airline in 1990, was seen visiting London–Gatwick in February 1990. *(Tom Singfield)*

1994 saw a repeat of the 'Visit Malaysia Year' seen in 1990. Boeing 747-4H6 lines up at Hong Kong's Kai Tak Airport on 14 November 1994. *(Robbie Shaw)*

Miami Air
Miami Air were established in August 1990 as a privately-owned charter airline and commenced operations in October 1991. Based in Miami they fly international, regional and domestic passenger charters to the Caribbean, North, Central and South America using a fleet of seven Boeing 727-200 aircraft. One of these carries the markings of the Miami Marlins baseball team and was seen at Miami during August 1995. *(Martyn Cartledge)*

Merpati

Merpati Nusantara Airlines were formed by the Indonesian government in September 1962 as the second state airline, primarily to take over the internal network developed by the Air Force since 1958. In October 1978 the airline was taken over by Garuda although Merpati continue to operate under their own name. In 1967 the countries of Brunei, Indonesia, Phillipines, Malaysia, Singapore and Thailand joined forces to create ASEAN, the Association of South East Asian Nations. Twenty-five years later, in 1992, Merpati applied 'Visit Asean Year 1992' to their aircraft, as seen being worn by PK-MLS, one of two Lockeed L-382G Hercules flying with the airline at the time.

Mexicana

Mexicana can lay claim to being the fourth oldest airline in the world and the oldest in North America, having been formed on 12 July 1921 as Compania Mexicana de Transportes Aereos, and adopting the present name in August 1924. In 1982 Mexico was hit by an economic crisis and the government increased its holding from fourteen per cent to fifty-eight per cent taking control of the airline. In August 1989 twenty-five per cent of their shares were sold and a new board of directors took control. One of their first duties was to create a new corporate image and the idea was established to give each aircraft its own individual livery based on the country's traditions, culture, art and crafts. After the delivery of their ninth A320 in July 1992 it was considered to be costly to apply a different livery to each tail and so a total of eight different schemes were repeated throughout the fleet. Some observers have unkindly nicknamed the tail patterns the 'wallpaper tails'.

XA-MCX Boeing 727

XA-MED Boeing 727 (Author's Collection)

The first aircraft to wear the new image, Boeing 727 N1279E, emerged during December 1990. Illustrated are some of the aircraft showing the variations in design and colour. During 1996 the airline celebrated its seventy-fifth anniversary and appropriate markings were added to the noses of each aircraft in the fleet. *N225RX Airbus A320 (author's collection)*

XA-RZU Airbus A320 (Author's collection)

XA-CUN Boeing 727 (Peter Cooper)

F-OHMJ Airbus A320
(Mark Daniels)

Boeing 727
(Mark Daniels)

F-OHMJ Airbus A320
(75th Badge)
(Mark Daniels)

N441LF Airbus A320
(Richard Vandervord)

F-OHMH A320 (with 75th badge)
(Derek Hellman)

Overseas National

During 1976 America celebrated the bicentenary of its independence and numerous military aircraft had special markings applied to record the event. One airline, Overseas National, also entered into the spirit of the occasion by decorating two of their DC-8s. Both aircraft had appropriate registrations and schemes with N1776R wearing a scheme based on the current US flag while its stablemate, N1976P, wore the Confederate flag of two hundred years earlier. The aircraft were later flown by the travel club Club USA International, and continued to carry the schemes for several years after the celebrations. N1976P was seen at Dallas–Fort Worth as late as 1982. *(Will Blunt) (N1976P - Confederate flag) (Author's Collection) (N1776R - Current US flag)*

Qantas – Wunala Dreaming

Ranking as one of the leading contenders for the most flamboyant scheme ever to grace an airliner, the Qantas Boeing 747-438, VH-OJB *Wunala Dreaming* would surely by hard to beat. Rolled out at Sydney on 3 September 1994, *Wunala* (Aboriginal for kangaroo) *Dreaming* tells the story of spirit ancestors in kangaroo form and blends ancient aboriginal art motifs with state-of-the-art aviation technology. The work of the Balarinji Design Studio in Adelaide, the design was digitised on computer and magnified one hundred times. Painted around the clock over thirteen days, the design features, 1,324 irregular dots, uses seven different colours and took eight hundred litres of paint. Following its roll-out the aircraft entered service the following day operating Qantas's inaugural service to Osaka–Kansai. *Wunala Dreaming* was seen a London–Heathrow in August 1995.

A close-up of the nose shows one of the kangaroos and many of the 1,324 dots that help form the design. *(SPA Photography)*

Qantas

At the opposite end of the special scheme spectrum to *Wunala Dreaming*, Qantas have also applied stickers to their aircraft on occasions. In 1993 'Sydney 2000' stickers were worn to help promote Sydney's successful campaign to host the Olympic Games in the year 2000. Also contesting for the rights were Manchester, England and Berlin, Germany. Whether the Qantas stickers had any influence on the final decision is doubtful but, that aside, the Australian city was the eventual winner of the bid. The 'Longreach' name on the nose not only represents the Boeing 747-400's range but is a reference to the airline's birthplace in Queensland.

Qantas holds the distinction of being the world's oldest airline, having been formed on 16 November 1920 as The Queensland and Northern Territories Aerial Services, which was soon shortened to Qantas, originally flying as an aerial taxi and joyride operation in the outback using a single war-surplus Avro 504K. In 1936 their first overseas service was introduced to Singapore with DH86 aircraft, a larger version of the Dragon Rapide. The 1940s saw Catalinas and Constellations fly for the airline and in 1959 the airline took delivery of the first non-US airline Boeing 707 to enter the jet age. Today Qantas fly 137 aircraft to almost 100 destinations.

In 1995 the airline celebrated its seventy-fifth anniversary and applied celebratory marks to all of its aircraft, as seen here on this Boeing 747. *(Mark Daniels)*

Ryanair – Christmas Schemes

A seasonal Christmas scheme has been adopted by many airlines in recent years and Ryanair have applied some festive spirit to their aircraft on more than one occasion. In 1994 their Boeing 737 fleet was treated to a Father Christmas face with each face being, reportedly, slightly different from the others. Boeing 737-200, EI-CJE, is seen departing from an equally seasonal Luton Airport on 2 January 1995. A close-up of the same aircraft was taken at Gatwick a few days earlier. The following year the fleet of eleven aircraft was again given the Christmas treatment when a beaming grin with party novelty, red nose and Christmas hat were worn on the nose of the aircraft. Photographed at Gatwick on 14 January 1996 was Boeing 737-200, EI-CKS, which is also the only aircraft to carry large bill-board-style Ryanair titles. *(Robbie Shaw- below)*

Ryanair Stansted–Glasgow

If you have a new service to promote then one way of getting the word across is to advertise on your own aircraft. Several airlines have adopted this promotional method and Ryanair were no exception when they wanted to publicise their new service from London–Stansted to Glasgow–Prestwick. One Boeing 737-200, EI-CJD, was painted with a tartan scarf wrapped around the cockpit and a grinning mouth on the aircraft's nose, a sight more reminiscent of the shark's mouth more commonly worn by military fighters. The service was also advertised on the rear fuselage. It was captured departing Stansted in the late autumn afternoon light on 5 November 1995 bound for Prestwick on one of four daily flights.

Sierra Expressway
Sierra Expressway were an Oakland, California-based regional airline formed in August 1995 to feed Southwest's and United Shuttle's Oakland operations. Flying a fleet of seven BAe Jetstream 31s they added special markings to one of these aircraft, N853JX, in late 1995 to promote the Monterey Aquarium. The beaver applied to the aircraft was seen posing for the camera in mid-February 1996, just days before the airline ceased operations on 16 February.
(Eric Trum)

Singapore Airlines

Singapore Airlines can trace its origins back to 1947 when Malayan Airways was formed. Renamed Malaysian Airways in 1963 and Malaysia–Singapore Airlines in 1970, it took its present name in 1972 following the separation of Singapore from Malaysia. As well as operating Airbus A310s and Boeing 737s, the airline also operates one of the largest Boeing 747 fleets and are the largest operator of the Boeing 747-400 'Megatop' variant. It was probably appropriate, therefore, when Boeing rolled their 1,000th 747 off the Everett production lines on 10 September 1993, almost twenty-five years after the first 747 was rolled out on 30 September 1968, that this aircraft should fly in Singapore colours. Commemorating the aircraft's historic milestone 9M-SMU proudly wears '1,000th Boeing 747' on the nose. The aircraft was seen on the gate at Heathrow in December 1995. *(SPA Photography)*

The aircraft was also seen at Zürich in June 1994. *(Olav Rheusius)*

The aircraft is seen departing from Los Angeles in February 1996. *(Mark Daniels)*

Southwest – Lone Star 1, Arizona 1 & California 1

On 6 November 1990, Southwest unveiled the first of three State Flag schemes when Boeing 737-3H4, N352SW, was delivered to the airline at Austin, Texas in the colours of the Texas state flag. Known as *Lone Star 1* the idea originated from Southwest's advertising agency, GSD & M Advertising of Austin, who thought it would be a good idea to pay tribute to the airline's home state for their twentieth anniversary in 1991. This idea was followed up on 23 May 1994 when N383SW was rolled out at Phoenix, wearing the Arizona flag and named *Arizona 1*. A third 737 appeared at Sacramento on 11 August 1995, *California 1*, N609SW, making its debut. Southwest are the nation's fifth largest airline with an all-737 fleet of about 240 aircraft currently serving forty-nine cities in twenty-three states.

Lone Star 1 (top and centre left) was seen while visiting Los Angeles in March 1996. *(Mark Daniels)*

Lone Star 1 (below) was seen about to depart Phoenix on 27 March 1996.

Southwest's second flag scheme, *Arizona 1*, (above) was seen preparing for departure in February 1996. *(Eric Trum)*

Arizona 1 (bottom right) was photographed during a late afternoon visit to Phoenix on 27 March 1996.

Southwest's third flag scheme features the bear of the California state flag and was photographed in January 1996.
(Derek Hellman)

Southwest – Sea World

In 1988 Southwest struck up a relationship with Sea World and on 23 May 1988 *Shamu I*, representing their Official Sea World Airline status, was unveiled on N334SW with a low flight over the Sea World Texas site in San Antonio. Two more Shamu schemes were to follow when N507SW, *Shamu II*, appeared on 30 May 1990 to represent Sea World of California, and N501SW, *Shamu III*, was rolled out on 7 September 1990 to represent Sea World of Ohio. The shape of the Boeing 737 perfectly portrays the shape of the killer whale, with the airline's trivia factsheet revealing that the 737 Shamu is 1,928 per cent heavier than the real thing at 135,000 pounds and 6.875 times longer at 110 feet. The aircraft required forty-eight gallons of white paint, thirty gallons of black and eighteen gallons of paint in Southwest's colours to achieve its appearance. Sea World of Texas was seen at Dallas Love Field in July 1988, while 'California' was also seen at Love Field in February in 1991, and 'Ohio' was seen on approach to Las Vegas in November 1995. *(Andrew Abshier) (Texas & California) (Bob Holder) (Ohio)*

Southwest – Number 1 Heart

The heart with the number '1' appears on all Southwest's aircraft except for the special schemes and represents the airline's first-place ranking amongst all major US airlines in on-time performance, baggage handling and customer satisfaction (fewest consumer complaints), after statistics published by the US Department of Transportation. These are known as the 'Triple Crown'. In 1992 Southwest won all three categories and in honour of the achievement decided to apply the heart, which represents the heart of Southwest's employees, to all of its aircraft for one year. Southwest repeated the accomplishment in 1993, 1994 and 1995. They will continue to be worn until at least February 1997 when the 1996 results are released.

The heart is seen being proudly worn on Boeing 737 N698SW.

Southwest – Spirit of Kitty Hawk

Southwest Airline's first routes were allegedly conceived on a paper napkin with a simple triangular drawing connecting Dallas (Love Field), Houston (Hobby) and San Antonio. Flights commenced on 18 June 1971 with a fleet of just three Boeing 737s. Six years later the fleet had slowly grown to six aircraft. Today the fleet still uses the Boeing 737 with a mixture of 200, 300 and 500 models and totals about 240 aircraft. The *Spirit of Kitty Hawk* name was applied to N300SW, Southwest's first 300 series aircraft, and was unveiled at 10.35a.m. on 17 December 1994. The naming commemorated the Wright brothers' historic first flight from Kill Devil Hill, Kitty Hawk, North Carolina exactly eighty-one years earlier, when Orville Wright flew the Wright Flyer 36.5 metres on a flight lasting twelve seconds, and in doing so made the first man-powered flight by a heavier-than-air aircraft. Two other aircraft, N301SW and N302SW, also wear the same name.

Swissair – 700th Anniversary of the Swiss Federation

The year 1991 saw the 700th anniversary of the Swiss Federation which prompted Swissair to carry a special logo to commemorate the milestone. The year also saw the airline celebrate its own sixtieth birthday. Formed in March 1931 by the amalgamation of two airlines, Ad Astra and Basler Luftverkehrs AG (Balair), the fleet consisted of sixteen aircraft. In 1934 they placed an order for the Douglas DC-2 and have continued to buy the company's aircraft ever since, with the MD-11 and MD-81 forming the modern link. Other current types include the Airbus A310, A320 and A321, Boeing 747 and Fokker 100, and between them they carry the Swissair name to 125 cities in sixty-seven countries. MD-11 HB-IWB, one of thirteen in the Swissair fleet, was seen at Zürich on 4 May 1991 wearing the 700th anniversary logo. *(Akinobu Okuda)*

Swissair – Farewell to the DC-10

The McDonnell Douglas DC-10-10 first appeared over twenty-five years ago making its first flight on 29 August 1970 with American Airlines, making the first scheduled flight on 5 August the following year. On 5 June 1972 the DC-10-30, an extended-range variant for intercontinental routes with more powerful engines, a third main undercarriage and increased wingspan, made its maiden flight. Deliveries began in November with KLM and Swissair being the first recipients. After almost twenty years' service and with 800,000 flying hours without incident

Swissair said farewell to the DC-10 as the type was phased out and replaced by the MD-11. One aircraft, HB-IHI, which joined Swissair in October 1977, was selected to wear a farewell message. Initially reading 'Farewell DC-10 21 May 92', this was changed to '22 May' the following day before finally reading 'Farewell DC-10' without the date. Despite these dates being applied, the type operated its final flight on 6 June 1992 when it flew Montreal–Zürich. The aircraft now flies with Northwest Airlines. *(Olav Rheusius)*

Transavia

It would seem that some airlines are happy for any excuse to apply additional markings to their aircraft. While Varig produced special markings to celebrate their country's victory in the 1994 Football World Cup, Transavia were just happy to celebrate their country's participation in the competition. Two of their three Boeing 757-200s, PH-TKB and PH-TKC, were treated to a number of football stickers bouncing along the fuselage. A total of twelve 757s are currently in the process of delivery to the airline and will fly alongside a similar number of 737s in the fleet. Corfu was the location on this occasion for PH-TKB in September 1994.
(Author's Collection)

TWA

Rolled out at Kansas City on 2 September 1994, TWA unveiled a different form of special scheme when MD-83, EI-BWD, appeared in a reverse scheme to their normal colours. Named *Wings of Pride* this aircraft was also different in that it was sponsored by the employees, who own forty-five per cent of the airline, and pay the lease payments on the aircraft through voluntary payments, in recognition of the airline's re-emergence after twenty-one months in bankruptcy. Anybody seeing the aircraft is made fully aware of this as the titles 'Sponsored by the Employee-Owners of TWA' are carried along the fuselage.
(Andrew Abshier)

Varig

Varig, or Viacão Aerea Rio-Grandense to give them their full title, were Brazil's first airline having been formed and commencing operations on 7 May 1927. Founded by a German immigrant, Otto Ernst Meyer, their first routes covered just southern Brazil. Today that service network has grown to a network serving thirty-five domestic destinations and thirty-one abroad in Central and South America, North America, Europe, Africa and Asia. Brazil is also know globally as a great exponent of football and in 1994 the world was once again reminded of this nation's footballing pedigree when they beat Italy in the final to win the World Cup held in the USA. Commemorating the occasion Varig dressed up one of their DC-10-30s, PP-VMD, with a green and yellow sash around the fuselage

Western Pacific

Western Pacific must surely have the most colourful fleet of any airline flying today with an all-Boeing 737-300 fleet, the majority of which fly as flying billboards on low-cost flights from Colorado Springs, Colorado to about twenty US cities coast-to-coast. Formed by Ed Beauvais, who also formed America West in 1981, the airline began operations on 28 April 1995. Western Pacific, or WestPac as they are often called, refer to their aircraft as logojets and have made the entire fleet available to any prominent corporations as flying billboards. The idea is not only to earn valuable revenue for the airline but also to put some fun into flying. By the end of 1996 the airline expects to have a fleet of twenty-four aircraft. The Broadmoor Hotel, a five-star hotel based in Colorado Springs since 1918 and offering 'European Grandeur in the Rockies', was the first company to invest in the idea. The hotel is owned by Edward Gaylord who is also an investor in Western Pacific. This aircraft flew WestPac's first flight on 28 April 1995 'on a service from Colorado Springs to Oklahoma City. Leased from USAir, the aircraft joined the airline as N501AU, but is now registered N947WP.

The second aircraft to take up corporate-sponsorship was Fox Television, who produce the popular cartoon series *The Simpsons*. Leased in May 1995 this ex-US Air machine first flew as N302AU before taking up the registration N949WP. The aircraft has been nicknamed the 'Electric Banana' and features *The Simpsons* characters along the fuselage and tail: Marge, mum in the family, graces the tail, while Bart and his dad, Homer, feature on the rear of the fuselage. Lisa and Maggie, sucking a dummy, share the forward fuselage. The aircraft was unveiled on 18 May 1995 at Hollywood-Burbank Airport, near the Fox studios.

With Colorado Springs being the home of Western Pacific, and Colorado's second largest city after Denver, the city took the opportunity to become the third logojet customer and dressed-up one of WestPac's aircraft to promote the popular ski resort and its attractions. The rear of the fuselage features the city's most prominent landmark, the 14,110-foot mountain known as Pike's Peak named after Lt. Zebulon Pike who, with a small detachment of soldiers, was the first white man to discover the mountain in 1806. Colorado Springs was named in 1871 after people began flocking to the area in 1859 in search of gold. Below Pike's Peak is another local landmark, the beautiful 'Garden of the Gods'. The aircraft, N951WP, was rolled out on 24 July 1995 after briefly wearing provisional 'Future Logo Jet' titles.

Unveiled in August 1995 to become the fourth logojet, N952WP, previously N503AU, also wears a scheme with a local connection, in this case the Colorado Technical College. Decked out in a predominantly blue and yellow scheme, the rear of the fuselage features a thirty-foot-long eagle and the college motto 'Soar to meet your Destiny'.

The Stardust Resort and Casino from Las Vegas are responsible for the stunning image of showgirl 'Oki' whose scantily clad thirty-seven-foot-tall body adorns the tail of the aircraft. The aircraft entered service on 15 November 1995 flying the inaugural WestPac service to Newark. Allocated the registration N950WP, but still wearing N301AU, the aircraft briefly flew with 'Beat the System' billboard titles after its delivery in July 1995. The titles refer to WestPac's advertising slogan. 'The System says all airlines are created equal. Western Pacific says 'Beat the System'. *(Author) (Stardust) (Andrew Abshier) (Beat the System)*

The least colourful aircraft in the Western Pacific fleet is 'WestPac Willie' which wears a provisional scheme promoting the airline's own cargo service. Delivered as N509AU in November 1995 and subsequently registered N953WP, the aircraft wears a natural finish with a cartoon Boeing 737 on the fuselage and the standard Western Pacific tail scheme.

Taking advantage of the chance to have their own logojet Western Pacific unveiled ex-Air Europa 737-319, N960WP, wearing 'Western Pacific' titles in billboard guise during late 1995. Featuring 'Western' in large red letters and 'Pacific' in blue letters, both sides of the tail are given one colour each with a red tail on the port side and blue on the starboard side.

Delivered just in time for Christmas 1995 Western Pacific lost no time in entering the festive season with a 'Winter Wonder Plane' scheme promoting the airline's Winter Wonder low-fare promotion. The aircraft featured a red nose (though this later changed to white) with a thirty-seven-foot-long Santa being pulled by a reindeer-horned WestPac Willie, the cartoon 737 nicknamed by the employees. Registered N962WP, the aircraft entered service on 15 December 1995 and was previously registered SE-DLO. With a change of season the Winter Wonder promotion gave way to the Spring Fling promotion. The Winter Wonder Plane was accordingly repainted to become the Spring Fling Jet.

Delivered on 24 October 1995 and unveiled on 14 November the following month N961WP was rolled out wearing a bright blue and white scheme advertising 'Thrifty Car Rental'. Entering service the next day on the airline's inaugural flight to Tusla the ex-Air Europa aircraft will wear the colours for four years. The tail of the aircraft shows 'Lenny the Caveman' who represents Thrifty's 'historically low rates'.

Rolled out on 22 March 1996, the Bronco Buster is the logojet of another local concern, 'The Professional Rodeo Hall of Fame', which is situated on the northern outskirts of Colorado Springs. Previously flying with TACA of El Salvador the aircraft, N375TA, carries the titles of the 'Professional Rodeo Cowboys Association' on the port side with the rodeo rider Ty Murray on the tail in blue and 'ProRodeo Hall of Fame' on the starboard tail, with a twenty-five-foot-high image of the rodeo rider Casey Tibbs, whose statue sits outside the museum.

Illustrated are some of the logojets lined up on the gates at their Colorado Springs base in March 1996.

The Thrifty and Rodeo aircraft take time out on the ramp at Colorado Springs. The Rocky Mountains form the backdrop for the photo.